PROMISING THE MOON

Going The Distance To Deliver

Gregory Cox

Copyright © 2015 Gregory Cox
All rights reserved.

ISBN: 069246798X
ISBN 13: 9780692467985

LET US PRAY

Lord God, we thank You for everything You've done in our lives. We thank You, Lord, that You are a God who knows all about us. You know our setbacks and our failures. We want to thank You for Your healing power. You are a God who heals Your people from alcoholism and drug addiction and all types of neglect and abuse. We thank You, right now, God.

Lord God, we ask that the readers of this book will feel Your Presence while they read, in spite of what they're going through. We pray, in the Name of Jesus, that healing will take place in their minds, in their bloodline, and in the lives of their children. We pray against any generational curses.

Thank you, God, for setting us up and preparing us for what we're about to do and where we are about to go. Heal all the women who have been abused by others. Give them direction and safety.

Let Your people make it to their destination, and in the midst of the mess and the madness, we pray that You will develop a message out of it, in the Name of Jesus. Open our minds and open our eyes to receive that which You have started.

Thank You for my life and everything You allowed me to go through so others can see the victory. We thank You, we honor You, and we bless Your Name. In Jesus Name, Amen.

DEDICATION

I want to dedicate this book to fatherhood, DCFS birth parents, and DCFS staff who are passionate about reuniting parents with their children.

I want to dedicate this book to foster parents who open their heart and home to children in need of love and care.

I want to dedicate this to those in substance abuse treatment and recovering from addictions.

I also want to dedicate this to my wife, Hattie, my children, close friends, and all the strong men who helped me become the man that I am today, especially my pastor.

- Gregory Cox

ACKNOWLEDGEMENT

I would like to thank my wife, Hattie, for listening to me and being there for me when I experienced anxiety about writing this book.

I would like to thank my sons and daughters for allowing me to be the father that I am today. I love you all.

I want to thank Pastor John F. Hannah for all of his encouragement, direction and wise counsel.

I want to thank Deborah Henry of Fresh Look Communications LLC, who helped me get this book ready for publication.

FOREWORD

Promising The Moon is a catalyst for those who not only desire to do better, but who recognize the need to be better. It is with great simplicity and honesty that Greg Cox invites you on his journey of recovery.

Promising The Moon is a great resource and inspiration for anyone facing the challenges of recovering from drug addiction.

Tonette Dugar - Author of *My Gift Of A Broken Heart*

CONTENTS

Let Us Pray	iii
Dedication	v
Acknowledgement	vii
Foreword	ix
A Time To Tell	1
Substance Abuse: Changed Behavior	3
Things Got Worse Before They Got Better	6
Domestic Violence	8
Camp Experience: Wandering Off Course	11
Fatherhood: The Relationship	16
Blended Family: Integrating With Love	21
Sons: The Next Generation	28
Emotional Rollercoaster: Life's Challenges	30
Real Life	32
Making Good Decisions	34
Lessons From My Pastor, Pastor John F. Hannah	36
Losing A Dream	49
Turning 50	54
Personal Integrity	56
Current Situation, Then And Now	58
Clicking The Links	60
Advocating For Others	62
Advocating With The Right Information	66
Quitting Is Not An Option	68
Courage To Seek Help	70
Slips And Setbacks	73
Inside Long-Term Recovery	76
About The Author	83

A TIME TO TELL

I was a guest speaker at a Lake County Treatment Center, speaking to birth parents who had open DCFS cases, who were seeking to get their children out of the system. It had as much of an impact on me as it had on them. I wasn't crunched for time and wasn't pressured about the number of attendees. I was able to deliver to the birth parents without professional or personal restrictions.

I recognize when people go on vacation, and when they return, things are so clear. I experienced that. I was able to return from vacation and share with the birth parents and give them what they needed. It was draining, but the next day I was light as a feather.

When I was coming up, my mother said, "What goes on in this house, stays in this house. Don't tell your business." We would get in trouble if we told.

She would also say, "If I'm not here, don't open the door for anybody. You can't have any company."

Even if she knocked on the door, I still checked the peephole to be sure she was who she said she was.

I was thinking about calling this book, I'm Telling. When our mouths have been muted not to say anything, it's because it was a practice and behavior from so long ago to avoid getting in trouble.

I asked my wife, Hattie, if the practice of not telling spills into our adult lives. We're hiding things we don't want the family to know because of embarrassment.

There were people who lived down the hall from us who had a child who was retarded. We didn't have terms of mental illness back then. They didn't allow people to come into their home because of the embarrassment of raising a child who was mentally and physically delayed.

I wonder how much of that carried over into my adult life? I couldn't tell my experiences of guilt and shame of what was going on because I was taught what goes on in the house stays in the house. Don't go running your mouth. Sometimes we're threatened not to tell. We didn't tell our personal business to avoid being judged or disliked. So, I would hide that my father was a drunkard, an addict and looked like the community clown if I saw him on the street. It was embarrassing to me to have a father who was unacceptable to some in the community, and for others, a fun person to be around.

We don't always say to people what needs to be said. I want to be exposed in the pages of this book. Even in this city, young people say they're not telling, they're not snitching. We need to get to the point. Get to the bullet point. We avoid and neglect getting help because we're not supposed to tell anybody, and it affects us later in life with a spouse, getting a job, or in relationships.

I'm exposing and telling on myself. I'm a mature adult now and can say what I want to say. This book is to help and motivate someone else to tell their story.

SUBSTANCE ABUSE: CHANGED BEHAVIOR

My substance abuse started at age thirteen. My mother died when I was thirteen. I had been smoking marijuana and drinking. My mother was in and out of the hospital with lung cancer and we had a lot of issues in the home. My sister was rebellious, my brother was using drugs and getting in trouble, and my father was promiscuous, using dope and acting out. There was a lot of domestic violence in the home. I didn't know this then, but I was using dope to mask everything that was going on.

My family had parties in the house and afterward there were open cans of Schlitz and Budweiser. I drank out of those cans, liking the fizz and the aftertaste. I didn't realize I was getting high.

It was easy to get marijuana then. It was cheaper. You could spend three dollars, get a bag of marijuana and roll sixteen joints out of it. Five dollars got you twenty-two joints. They sold joints for a dollar or two.

I can say my drug use took off during that time, not understanding what my mother was going through during that period. Now that I've been clean and sober all these years, I can look back now and see her struggles, including her daughter, oldest son, husband, and her health problems. This is when my substance abuse began. When my mother died, I went to her funeral, high.

My grandmother (our relative care provider) lived on the West Side and it was recommended that we move in with her, but I refused to go. I wanted to stay in the projects with my father. My aunt wasn't hearing that. She told me to go to my grandmother's house, and eventually I went.

When my grandmother died, my aunt, my mother's sister, raised us. I was still getting high and grieving the loss of my mother. I lived in another set of the projects, and was the new kid on the block. I found the teenagers who were getting high and started hanging out with them. We used a little cocaine back then, but not a lot because the popular drug was happy sticks. I went from marijuana to happy sticks, which was sherm sticks or PCP. A sherm stick was a More cigarette dipped in happy stick water and wrapped in aluminum foil. We would smoke it and it was a trip.

I dropped out of school and moved in with an older woman upstairs on the 11th floor. My aunt told me not to be a kept man. She wanted me to be my own man. It stunts a man's growth to be taken care of by women. It's not healthy. It's creating a lazy man who thinks everybody is supposed to take care of him and he doesn't have to do anything for himself.

For me, it was unhealthy to be taken care of by women. Men need to experience being on their own and paying their own bills before moving in with someone. It should be a team effort, and they need to know their part in paying the expenses. I don't recommend moving in with women, anyway, because they can get mad, put you out and say, "This is my house!"

I moved out of my aunt's apartment, moved in with someone else, still drinking and drugging, and not working. I didn't want to work and wasn't even looking for work in my early twenties, thinking I was invincible. A man's growth is hindered when someone is doing everything for him.

I left the older lady, and me and my son's mother moved out of the projects and into an apartment on the West Side of Chicago, the same block where my grandmother used to live, right down the street. I would often go back to my old neighborhood to my old hang outs. My son's mother was taking care of me, getting a large Public Aid check and it was the same thing again. She was getting $700 or $800 a month in food stamps and cash. The rent was $35 or $45 a month, depending on your income.

After having our son and going for a six week checkup, she discovered she was pregnant again. That went on four years. Some of my kids are nine months apart. I had eight children by her.

THINGS GOT WORSE BEFORE THEY GOT BETTER

I started using cocaine. We were drinking. The addiction took off and got worse. With the addiction you start losing relationships and kids. Everything began to dwindle. We weren't paying bills, not buying much food, not buying clothes for the kids because that would mean spending the drug money. We sold food stamps to get drugs.

A DCFS child protection investigation was done. All the kids were removed from us by DCFS and placed in the care of her mother, their grandmother. DCFS found out because she had a premature baby, the baby had drugs in his system and we weren't going to the hospital to visit him. The baby died.

When I tell this story, I admit I was wrong and neglected my parental responsibilities. I went to get substance abuse treatment and do what I had to do to reunite with my children. We both agreed to go into treatment in March 1991 and get our babies back. That was the plan but it didn't work out that way. She had her slips and setbacks and went back to using. I was disappointed, but stayed in treatment, stayed in the facility, getting stronger and healthier.

When people get clean and sober, sometimes they have slips and setbacks, but that's not true in all cases. I was able to leave the facility one Thanksgiving to go to my aunt's for dinner. My brothers were there, drinking. It was the first time I was tested being at a social gathering and not drinking. My aunt was rooting for me to stay clean because she had raised me. She didn't want me to stay at her house long, but get back to the center. She'd seen all of her sister's kids suffering from alcoholism and drug addiction. She probably wished she could have done more for us. She encouraged me and admired the fact that I stayed clean. My life continued to improve.

Sometimes I call my aunt to tell her how much I love her and appreciate her for putting her life on hold to take care of us.

DOMESTIC VIOLENCE

I was a perpetrator of domestic violence. The things I saw my father do, I began to do the same things. I hit my kids' mother. There are signs and symptoms of domestic violence. Men seek out their victims. They hit women to see how they will accept it. They will push to see if you'll push back. They will test you to see the response. If there's no response, if you're not going to hit back, not going to call the police, and you're going to take it, it increases. As the violence increases, fear increases. I sensed her fear of me, so I would continue to hit her.

I'm a punk. I wouldn't fight men, but would hit my women. I've shared this at men's groups. My mother was a victim of domestic violence, my sister was a victim, and now her daughter, my niece. This is the third generation of this spirit. I've been married twenty years and have never hit my wife, Hattie. Early in our marriage, I tested her. I grabbed her arm, squeezed it, and she grabbed my arm back. I was like, okay; that's a wrap. That was the end of that.

There was some built up anger in me from the death of my mom at a young age. I loved my father and I ended up being just like him, which was crazy. A few of the things he did was good, like telling me to save money, but the majority of what he did wasn't healthy, like using dope and being promiscuous. There was stirred up anger in me and I took it out on whoever I could. I abused them and it appeared to them that it was okay for me to do that. I was a perpetrator, and out of anger and because I could control them, I put fear in them to make them do what I wanted.

My father had that spirit in the house which resulted in fear. My father tore my house up, physically, spiritually and emotionally. That spirit ran through my house and my aunt's house. When my parents fought, tables were thrown all over the room, my mother was thrown all over the room, glass was broken, and after the police were called, they would tell him to leave. We would leave and go to her mother's house, and when we returned we had to put things back together like nothing happened. Then she would let him back in and he would do it again. I remember picking up chairs, glass and pots to make the house look normal, and it wasn't. That was a critical time for me. I was young then.

I found out from my aunt that when my mother took sick, my father came back and took care of her. I didn't know that. The last time I saw her was on a Saturday. I was in the bed, in the projects, looking at cartoons. My father had her in his arms. I asked where they were going and my mother said she would be back, she was going to the hospital. She never came back.

In my mind, because of the abuse, I blamed him and felt he took her away from me, associating the abuse with her in his arms. I didn't know that he had come back to take care of her. I respected him later for doing that, but knew he probably did it out of shame and guilt from all of the abuse.

Domestic violence, victims and perpetrators have been in my bloodline. When I got off dope, I was delivered from it. I don't talk about this unless I'm on a panel and have a voice to speak about things like this. Men need to be educated more on when there is a trait of domestic violence in their family. Women need to know how to spot the signs of a perpetrator and find out where they got the idea that it's okay to be abused.

It's important to receive current information about domestic violence and educate yourself to recognize the warning signs.

CAMP EXPERIENCE: WANDERING OFF COURSE

After I finished treatment, I was enrolled in an eighteen month transitional living program. Every year, Pastor Vince would take a group of guys on a week camp experience in Wisconsin. He asked me, and I took him up on his offer to go.

There were twenty men who were broken up into four groups of five. When we got to the campsite early in the day, the four groups were given an assignment to meet at the same location, but we were given different routes to get there before sundown. Our group wandered off course and got lost.

One of the guys in our group had bad feet that were really hurting. We all carried big camp bags with a tent and everything. Since his feet were hurting, he couldn't carry his stuff. We sat down and tried to figure out what we could do to help him. One guy suggested we take turns carrying his bag along with our own bag. Someone else made a better decision, for everyone to take something from his bag to carry. That made it lighter for him and he was able to get up and we got back on course.

It was a great experience for me to be a part of that group. I had never been to camp before. We got lost, but we got back on course, and was able to help a fellow camper who was getting weak and needed help carrying his load. I was glad we sat down as a group and took the time to help him. Sometimes we can wander off course and never ask someone for directions or help to bear the load.

This guy, in pain and getting blisters on his feet, was able to stop and say, I can't go any further. Once we took some of his things and the weight was off him, he was able to move a little faster. That camp experience showed me what it was like to be a team player when someone wanders off course.

I have to be careful not to wander off course from where God is taking me and what He is doing in my life. I can't have a heavy load and not know how to ask for help.

Every day there was a destination to reach, but along the way we had a lot of obstacles to overcome to reach the next place or the next phase. Every thirty minutes we reached another obstacle to go around to get to the next one.

One day, there was a rope tied from one end of a tree to the other tree and we had to walk a tightrope, walking across to the other end. We had a rope tied around our waist, in case we fell, to prevent us from hitting the ground. This was three stories high. There was one rope in the middle and two ropes on either side to hold on to while walking the tightrope to the other tree, where the ladder was. There were some guys who were scared to get on the tightrope, but everybody had to get over the tightrope as a team. Some of the men who crossed over, came down, then came back up to support another guy as he crossed over. Then he knew he wasn't alone.

I was early in recovery, just sixty or ninety days clean. Those different obstacles and challenges helped me with courage, support and to stay clean. While completing the obstacles, something rose in me to let me know I was strong, a winner and had the victory. We had a week of obstacles to overcome. On the last day we came together as men and faced larger obstacles because they were becoming more difficult.

There was a large spider web that we had to get through without knocking it down or tearing it up. One person would go through it and help the next one. It was challenging. Guys were crying, afraid, and frustrated. The obstacles were creating emotions I hadn't experienced in awhile because of the drugs. The feelings that were coming up had previously been masked with drugs and alcohol. I felt not only victory, but shame and guilt when I didn't do it the way I should have, and selfishness when I didn't help the next guy. But, I stayed the course.

Some guys couldn't make it through the week and went home because they had never been away from the city. Guys were getting sick and couldn't stay. There were guys who were afraid to stay because we were in a cabin in the woods, and those who were anxious, and couldn't complete the tasks. This experience strengthened and gave me the stability to want more recovery, change and power to conquer personal challenges that were hindering me from being successful. The camp experience was a first time being away from the norm, but it felt good to be away. I stopped smoking there. I took one cigarette to Wisconsin, smoked half of it and haven't looked back since.

We had personal time to go into the woods. I took a journal with me and accessed how, why and when I started smoking. I lived in the Rockwell projects and was hanging with a friend whose older brother hung around a lot of ladies and smoked cigarettes. He looked so cool. That's when I started smoking. I wanted to be cool too, and smoked from age thirteen to twenty seven. I wrote this down during the camp experience, which helped me become who I am today. I came back as a man, having tackled the fear of bugs, animals and the woods. I needed those positive successes. Even now, when I have victories, I can get that same feeling.

The guy who had an issue with his feet and couldn't walk the tightrope is still battling addiction to this day. He's been in treatment several times. The camp experience opened wounds for some. If you open a wound and can't close it, it gets infected. The camp experience traumatized him. A drug addict deals with trauma by medicating it with dope.

The eighteen month transitional program started with thirty guys in a dorm, ten guys in the middle and ten guys on each end. You had a bed, a nightstand, a wooden closet, and a community washroom. The program was in phases. This was the first phase. The second phase was going downstairs to a cubicle that had a bed, nightstand and a closet. You could stay out a little later. The next phase was around the corner to the Monroe Residence. You had a cubicle with a bed, nightstand and a tall dresser. You could come in when you got ready. After camp I went to the next phase where I continued going to my meetings and getting stronger. Camp really helped me.

There was a family shelter for women with children. Because I was trying to get my kids back from DCFS, I was granted unsupervised visitation. Then they gave me overnight visitation, but I had nowhere to take them. I went to the head of the shelter and told them I needed somewhere to take my kids for overnight visits. They talked to the director and I integrated the shelter as the first male in an all women and children's shelter. I paved the way for other men. I was a single father and this was the ideal place, where I stayed six months. After that, there was a program where you could move into an apartment and they would pay half your rent for a year. I moved out.

I was a single father for two years before I married my wife and she moved in with her kids. When my kids were with their grandmother, I wasn't worried about them. I thank God I took them up on the camp experience. It was life changing. I came back a man. Everything was uphill after that.

Everyone needs to have a camp experience. You may not have to go away for five days, but you need something that will mature you to be the best you can be. That's why I'm still with Pastor John Hannah. He pulled out of me what needed to be pulled so I could be the best that I could be.

FATHERHOOD: THE RELATIONSHIP

I was in treatment, got three of my boys back from the Department Of Children And Family Services, and moved into my own apartment, where I stayed six months. I had a part time job and stayed sober, raising three boys.

As a single father, I was responsible for cooking, cleaning, washing clothes, and allowing them to assist me in the housecleaning. The respect I had for single women shifted when I realized all they had to do.

I had a son who was a bed wetter, so I had to go to the Laundromat with sheets that were soaked with pee. We didn't have a washer in the building. Sometimes I had to wait a few days before I was able to go wash them. Ugh!

I had to wash, cook, help with homework, meet with teachers, take them and pick them up from school, and take them to the barbershop. Everything that I had neglected when I was using dope, I had to do with the first three boys I got back.

There were times I was proud to be a father. A movie had just come out about a father raising sons in an dangerous neighborhood. I was really trying to save my boys. They couldn't wear hats. They were between the ages of seven and ten. I had to teach them how to be boys. I wanted the best for them and was honored to be their father.

In the beginning, I was operating out of guilt and shame because I had left them and had used dope. I started out trying to give them everything they wanted like I was trying to make up for lost time. After I met my wife, Hattie, she told me I didn't owe them anything; I'd gotten clean and gotten them back. She told me, "Stop. You've already made things right."

I had to stop myself from buying them expensive things and began making sure their basic needs were met. They still got nice things, but it wasn't so important that they had the name brand things. What was important was that I was there for them as their father and wanted the best for them.

I didn't have a sitter, so I took them with me a lot. They went to the 12 Step meetings with me. Everybody knew and identified me as Greg, with the three boys.

It wasn't a challenge what I was doing; it was a challenge that I was doing it sober. I was cooking and cleaning, but now, I was by myself and wasn't drunk. I was doing everything with a sober mindset and was by myself. It felt really good. The house was clean, they were in the bed and I was playing some Jazz, feeling like God had blessed me and allowed me to have an opportunity to make right what was wrong. He put me back into position, and restored me, like Jesus restored Peter. He restored my life, free from drugs, and restored my fatherhood. It was like He was saying, take care of these boys and go get the rest of them. Not only that, but you will help other men take care of their boys. They will admire you for going back to get yours and taking care of them. My pastor told me he admired me for going to get my boys.

After the camp trip, treatment, and now, in my own place, this was a defining moment where fatherhood became clear and important to me. It's not about me; it's about these kids. Now, it's about helping other fathers and helping my sons who have their own kids, be great men. It's bigger than me.

My sons had their own challenges; some went to jail and had their own substance abuse issues, but they can honestly say that this man went back and got his life together, took care of his kids and gave them what they needed to be great men. I believe every one of my sons has what it takes to be a greater father and a great leader in their home. They all know how to cook. I cooked all the meals, made sure they had breakfast, sat at the doctor's office with them when they got sick, and all of this as a single father. It helped me be the person I am today.

My wife said the kids helped grow us up. She said they put the pressure on us to mature. They demanded that we be great parents. They depended on us to get it right, not to quit and not to fall back. We couldn't afford to blow it. We had to be the best parents that we could be. People respect us for that to this day.

It's important for a single father to learn everything a single mother does to make sure the children's needs are met. He has to humble himself to make sure all their needs are met because they're trusting him. That's the importance of being a father to children who were wounded, who were hurt, who were scarred, and who were damaged. My kids were all of that and they needed me to be there faithfully, and I was. Every man has to understand that he must be there for his children. I tell my sons this. Men must grow as fathers.

I did get some love from my father. Some of the great times we had together was watching old black and white movies. We would sit down and watch old cowboy and Indians and Army pictures. I didn't realize that those were our moments. I didn't see it back then. Those were intimate moments to watch all those old shows with my father.

My father was always on the go, in and out of the house, using drugs. He was always fighting my mother. He had to leave the house or we had to leave and go to her mother's house as a result of it. Then we had to come back and rearrange the house and put it back in order, like nothing happened.

I'm not sure what my kids would say our moments are, but I want them to have them. When they come to my house, sometimes I throw myself into their arms like I'm going to fall and they're responsible for holding me up. That's one of my moments. As fathers, we need those moments. My kids had to trust that I was going to be there and not go and get drunk, or smoke up and drink up everything in the house. I had to make sure that wasn't going to happen. Men must learn to take their position and how to keep that position.

When I met my wife, Hattie, she had four kids, so I had to be a father to her kids. They know me as their father. Her youngest daughter was three. She's twenty four now. Her sons were young but knew me as a man who stuck and stayed with their mother and showed them what it was to be a father. That came from being a single father and being able to identify with what mothers go through when they can't find the right man to help them raise their kids.

Parents have to be wise about who they let around their kids. At the time, I didn't know who I wanted around my kids, as a single father. I used to be promiscuous, so when I got sober and clean, it was all about me raising those boys. I didn't need someone who was hung up on jewelry and clothes; I needed someone who was going to be a mother to them.

God put Hattie in my life and she was a mother to my boys. She liked dressing, but it wasn't a high priority back then. My kids needed someone who was faithful to them, who was going to love them and not leave them. I wanted to make sure their emotional, physical, spiritual, and educational needs were met.

BLENDED FAMILY: INTEGRATING WITH LOVE

When Hattie and I got married, I was not the biological father of her children and she was not the biological mother of my children. This was bringing two families together with different experiences and some of the same.

When I think of a blended family, it's like a blender, where you're mixing stuff together. It's combining and integrating. I had just gotten out of treatment, was sober and trying to stay sober. I didn't have my kids back then. I was trying to regain custody of them. I ended up getting three of my sons back, so I was a single father with three kids. She was a mother of four but was living with her mother. We combined two families.

I'm third to the oldest and my wife is third to the oldest. We were in a position of bringing two families together. My kids came with a lot of anger, resentment, bitterness, and confusion because they had been in foster homes and were removed from us. My kids were more unhealthy than her kids were, because her kids had never been uprooted, and had always been with either the mother or the grandmother. Her kids weren't as wounded and scarred as mine. That was big to me. I can look back and see how we blended these families, how we hung in there and we stayed until the kids were adults. But, there were some challenges.

My kids had challenges with her being my wife. I had been a single father for two years and then my wife and her kids moved in with us. My kids were territorial. They had stuff that was theirs. I was territorial too. It was some time before I gave my wife some space in my closet. She had to remind me that we were married and living there together.

The kids moved in with us and my kids were mad. Her kids were messing with their stuff. Her kids did not have a challenge with me like my kids had with her. They accepted me and I accepted them. I knew that I was raising them and treating them all equal. It was hard for my kids to accept that they had someone there loving them. They had been separated from their mother, moved in with the grandmother, then separated from the grandmother and placed in foster homes. They had trust issues. My wife was loving on them and it was hard for them to accept the love because they'd been bounced around and still loved their own mama. They were trying not to disown their mother or push her to the back burner, and still have a relationship with Hattie. It was a struggle.

They would leave and spend the weekend with their mother and come back mad at my wife, treating her bad. But, she hung in there. Her kids didn't have a problem with me. We were cool. It got easier the longer we were together.

They tried to play us against each other. If her kids asked could they have cookies, and I told them no, they would go ask their mother. She would tell them yes, and they would come and sit in front of me with cookies. Wait a minute!

My kids would do the same thing. This was their house, their domain, so they were territorial with cereal, bowls, space, toys, and their room. Territorial. How we handled it was we sat them down and told them they had to ask both of us. If they didn't ask us both, the answer was no. If they asked me and I asked them what did their mother say and they said she said no, then the answer was no. We had to learn as a couple how not to take our own kid's side. If we did, there was a debate.

We were raising healthy kids with unhealthy, wounded kids. It was like kids in an orphanage who have all experienced something different, but lived together. You're trying to love them all, and some accept it and some don't because they don't believe it's authentic, that there must be something behind it.

We blended our kids together and loved them all equally and eventually the kids began to respect my wife. I had to tell them, "This is not your mother; she's my wife, but you will respect her because she's an adult and she's helping me take care of you."

It took awhile. They didn't want to disregard their mother because they loved their mother and did not want to disrespect her.

These kids are grown and have kids of their own now. It was destined for me and Hattie to be together.

There are challenges in blended families. Hattie had challenges with my kids' mother. I told her she could talk to my wife and she would convey any message to me. I never had a challenge with her kids' father, except one day he called the house and I answered the phone. I'm wondering, why is he calling my house? A spirit of jealousy rose up, but I had to talk to him. We worked through it. My wife and I had gotten so healthy that she would drop the kids off to their mother's and I would drop his kids off to him. We had to show them that we were working together as a team, just as we had to show the kids.

My wife had two daughters and I didn't have daughters. That gave me an opportunity to raise girls. My daughters love me. They were three and five when we got married. I was able to raise girls and do the father-daughter thing and love them and show them what a father was, staying there and making sure all their needs were met. My wife showed my sons what a mother looks like, someone who loves and won't leave. Her kids can understand and have compassion for someone who has been through some challenges and my kids can have compassion and love for someone who has had a different experience.

My sons will be good fathers. My daughters know what to look for in a father. Will they do that or not? They say a girl looks for her father and a boy looks for his mother. I want them to find someone they know is a team player. My sons have kids by women who already had kids. We accept all of those kids as our grandkids and my sons are accepting them as their kids too. Why? Because this is how they were raised. It's a blended family.

My daughters are responsible and don't require a lot of support. They understand the importance of being employed.

I was wounded along with my kids in the blended family and had to go through my own personal healing as a man and a father. There was guilt and shame from abandoning my kids. My wife and I were getting healed at the same time in the process of combining these families.

I had a sponsor. A sponsor is someone who guides you through the program and helps you maintain sobriety and encourages you to attend meetings. The meetings were my outlet. I would go and talk of the frustration of being there and raising all these kids. At that time, we had seven kids with us and we were in our twenties. Three more kids came after that because I was gradually getting my other sons back. I have a total of nine sons.

I encourage men to be a part of a men's group. I had a men's group where I could talk about my frustrations of what I was doing, my fears of not wanting to do it and thinking I made the wrong decision.

During the 12 Step meeting I could talk about frustrations of trying to make things work and going to work. This was about shared parenting. Some days I'm going to do 80% and she's going to do 20%. Some days I'm going to do 30% and she's going to do 70%. Everyday I'm not going to be at the high end and every day I'm not going to be at the low end. I was a single father, so I did it all: cooked, cleaned, went to the Laundromat, went up to the school, went to the hospital, and all of that. I recommend that men and women in blended families join groups where they have an outlet. Kids and teens need an outlet too.

In blended families you worry if the kids like you. My aunt who raised me said that they may not like my wife, but they have to respect her, and out of the respect will come the love. She said, "Teach those boys how to respect her and they will grow to love her."

She was right. They really love her today. They tried to run her off in the beginning, wondering why Hattie and her children had to move in with them. My kids cherished the times we spent alone together. Spend times with your biological kids and vice versa. It's healthy, because they all have to realize that they're loved the same.

You have to know the strengths and weaknesses of your kids. Know where there's a void, where they need more affection, a listening ear, or more encouragement. Some kids are introverts and some are extroverts. Know what they need at different ages and stages of their life. When puberty started, I didn't do well at that. My focus was meeting their immediate needs: shelter, food and clothing. I didn't monitor or make it my business to focus on a lot of their development as they got older.

We were living in a two bedroom apartment when my wife moved in with us. There we were, with seven kids in a two bedroom apartment, and then we had to move. A friend of ours offered to let us move into his building and rent a three bedroom apartment on the second floor. The first time he asked, I said no. I couldn't do that. The next time he asked, I took him up on it. We moved upstairs from him.

He took us in when we had nowhere else to go, opening up his heart and building to us. It wasn't easy because we had seven young kids growing up. I was determined not to move into another apartment after that, and we didn't. We moved into a home eighteen months later. My friend died years after that. I loved him. He was a great friend. He admired me because of what I did to get my kids back. His wife knew my wife.

My focus back then was to pay bills, and make sure that the kids ate and had clothes. I realize, now, that the kids should have had family therapy. My focus was to keep working.

I had just gotten off drugs, didn't have a high school diploma, no GED, no degree. I was trying to work, pay for a house and raise our kids in my late twenties. But God! God moved. Every time it was time for a raise, God moved. As my kids got older and I needed a raise, God shifted me so that I would have what I needed for that season. The money we had was enough. Food wasn't expensive then. They weren't wearing name brand clothes.

This was the early nineties. As they grew, God placed me in different jobs every four or five years and gave me more money, without the education. It was all God. Nobody gets the credit for that. It was God.

SONS: THE NEXT GENERATION

Two of my sons came to visit. They're 29 and 30 years old. I talked to them about fatherhood and being a great father. When I met my wife she had four kids and these are two of her boys. When I met them, they were babies. I had an opportunity to talk with them. They both have sons and are living with the mother of the boys. I talked to them about the importance of working and saving and being great fathers.

That's one thing my father said to me a lot: save some money. He didn't do a lot of working, but always stressed, save some money. That always resonated with me: save some money. I tell my sons the same thing. As you work, save money so you will have something to fall back on. Try to put away something.

Business tells you that you need so many months of rent or mortgage in an account, just in case. Right? So, I had this conversation with them. It was just us. I told them, as fathers, sometimes you have to prioritize your spending.

I told my sons to save and put away not just for you, but for your family. You have to continue to save to meet their needs.

My pastor talked about that today, learning to manage what you have and not spend above your means.

I've been there. I didn't spend extensively because I wanted to save and make sure my basic needs were met. Sometimes I called them 'no meat weeks.' You just ate whatever was in the cabinet, even if it was bread, string beans and carrots. Learn how to manage the small things, so when you get the large things you can manage those too.

I told my sons, when me and your mother were raising you, I got paid for two weeks and was able to get a pack of boxers and a T-Shirt and was able to keep it moving for the next two weeks. They never knew that this is what I had to do to make sure they ate. What I learned as a father, I want to make sure my boys get it. Save, budget and don't try to run out there getting the latest stuff.

EMOTIONAL ROLLERCOASTER: LIFE'S CHALLENGES

Writing this book opened up emotions in me. Wounds were opened because some of these topics hadn't been touched since I was in therapy. I didn't realize how much I'd opened up about my mother struggling with being sick with cancer, my older brother and sister acting out and my father using dope and acting out. They're all deceased. It's hard to read this because there's so much information about my life in just one paragraph, and so many emotions attached.

I remember going to my brother's funeral mad as hell. I was mad because he and my sister put me in a position to be the older sibling, when in fact, they were the oldest. I was mad at them. They didn't give me a chance to be the little brother. They both died as a result of using drugs and alcohol. I believe one of many reasons God got me clean was to be able to make arrangements and bury them.

All my life I had to act like the oldest and care for my brothers under me. I think that's part of why I started using dope. I needed my own time and didn't want to have to take my little brothers with me everywhere I went. I felt like I was never able to be who I wanted to be. Of course, I forgave them, but I was mad. I know God chose, anointed, called, and raised me up to be who I am and who I am in the family. I know that now, but then, I didn't see it.

REAL LIFE

My brother and sister died two years apart. I wasn't quite finished grieving from my brother's death when my sister died. They were hang-out buddies. They lived in Gary.

When my brother died, I had to travel to Gary twice a week to make arrangements.

The day before the funeral they wanted the balance. I had to travel to make the payment and come back the next morning for the funeral. Two years after that, my son got murdered.

I've been trying to soak in all that I've been through and have overcome, and didn't realize how much of a weight that was. It shut me down and I had to work some things out in my head and pray. I wanted to talk to some friends to get my strength back, but none of my friends were available. There were times when I just needed to talk and share.

Therapy gave me the tools and strategies to cope with what happened. I learned not to over commit myself when my emotions are all over the place. I don't want to get distracted when I need to stay on course.

That's part of what the book is about; trying to sort out some things, encourage someone else and enlighten them about what I went through. I want to be stripped of everything I went through to help someone else. Whatever God put in me to help others, I want to be emptied of it before I die.

I want someone healed from this book. When I speak to DCFS and the professional people, I don't want to just tickle their ears. I want to impact change. I'm not looking for applause. I want someone to read this and say, this is how he got out and I can do it too.

MAKING GOOD DECISIONS

My father told me to save some money. I wonder, did he talk about saving money so he would have money the next day to get drugs, or was it just him saying, save money? I don't know why he said it, but the concept made sense. Me, being a kid, I'm like, what are you talking about? Saving nickels? We're talking about the seventies when there was penny candy and you could get two for a penny. It wasn't like I had to save a lot of money. If I saved a quarter for the next day, that was major. I don't know where he got that from, but now that I'm an older man, the concept of saving and putting away money to care for my family has a larger meaning to me. Part of that came from my father.

When I was using drugs, I saved money so I could wake up the next day and get more so I wouldn't be withdrawing half the day and I'd be able to get my hit and keep it moving. Is that how it worked for my father, or was he given that advice from his father? Well, it worked for me.

Men, as leaders, need to be open to hearing those messages from people in our lives to help us better ourselves and prepare for later. I never want to get to a point where I'm not able to hear what I need to hear to mature and get what I need for later. They may say it now and it may not have an impact, but later on, it can be understood.

My aunt told me my mother used to say, "Clothes don't make me; I make clothes." I didn't understand it at first, but what she meant was, no matter how good a pair of dress pants look, if nobody wears it, it has no value. You can look just as good in something inexpensive as in something expensive, depending on your attitude. I made the clothes look good.

LESSONS FROM MY PASTOR, PASTOR JOHN F. HANNAH

Somebody suggested I get involved with John Hannah when he was doing the youth ministry, I.Y.S.B.C. (Inner-City Youth Spring Break Conference). I was a youth minister in a small church, so I connected with him at I.Y.S.B.C., got involved and stayed involved.

I didn't know him real close, but his leadership inspired me. When he was leading IYSBC, he had ministers from different churches get together and we formed different committees. He came in, took leadership, and he owned that thing. That's the main thing that impressed me; his leadership of the youth conference.

Pastor Hannah organized a luncheon in a downtown hotel and invited a lot of the pastors from local Chicago churches. The reason for the luncheon was to ask the pastors to support the youth conference, because they were sending the youth, but weren't sending any money for the youth who were getting blessed.

He had some of the youth leaders on the IYSBC committee help him host and greet the people. Everyone was uniformly dressed in black. We had a big conference room, and we served them lunch. It was so elegant. I had never seen this before. I was like, this is where I want to be. The last IYSBC conference I attended was the largest one, at Navy Pier. It was awesome!

Meanwhile, I was at a church and felt, there's got to be more. I told my wife, Hattie, I was thinking about leaving, it's just not working, I'm not growing.

I was working in the juvenile court building with a social service agency as a recovery coach. At the time, Pastor Hannah was working for the juvenile detention center. I was in and out of the court building, just like he was.

I was in the court building for a week straight, looking for him. I was compelled to find him and ask what church he attended, because I was ready to move from the church where I was at the time.

Pastor Hannah found me before I found him. I was standing there talking to a case worker, and he touched me on my shoulder. The touch from his hand was so powerful, I still remember it today. I believe it was a divine connection. He touched me and I turned around and said, "Man, I've been looking for you!"

He said he was about to get planted. (At this time, he had left St. James Church and was with Pastor Choco at New Life Covenant).

He said, "I'm about to start a church." He gave me his number. I asked him what church he attended and he said he was in Humboldt Park at a Hispanic church. I asked him when was he there. He said, Wednesday Bible Study and Sundays.

I told my wife, and I went to the New Life Covenant Wednesday Bible Study. I went by myself and left my family at their church. I started going to Pastor Choco's Wednesday Bible Study and Sunday church services. I asked my wife to join me on a Wednesday at Pastor Choco's church. She liked it and she liked the praise team. She started going to Bible Study on Wednesdays, but to her church on Sundays.

Pastor Choco planted Pastor Hannah on the South Side to do a Bible Study on Thursdays. I started going to Thursday Bible Study, but to the Mother Church on Sundays. My wife came with me when we started the Bible Study on the South Side at the Blackwell Memorial AME Zion Church. We attended faithfully on Thursdays.

We were attending Bible Study on Thursdays at the AME church and Pastor Hannah started having Sunday services at the Charles Hayes Center.

My wife attended Sunday services with me. My teenagers were still at the old church, but I found out they were either going in late or wouldn't go to church at all because we left the house before they did. I told them they had two weeks to say their goodbyes. That church was down the street from where we lived.

Me and my boys set up the Charles Hayes stage for worship on Sundays. We would go to Pastor Hannah's house to get the key to get the equipment that was at the Blackwell church.

I had a van, and would take the seats out of my van and load up all of the equipment Sunday mornings to take it to Charles Hayes and set it up for 10:00 worship. When worship was over, we would break it down, load the van back up, take the equipment back to the church, give them the key and go home. We did this every Sunday. It was a blessing for me that my boys helped out setting up the stage.

Pastor often says he looks forward to the day we don't have to keep breaking down stages. My sons and I were the first crew to do that.

When my sons got older, they didn't want to participate, so Pastor Hannah went to a men's shelter and got some men from the shelter to help with the set up. I would continue to help them set the stage, but it got to the point where I was involved in other ministry activities with Pastor Hannah, so I was released from that.

That whole process helped me to stay focused, to know that I was part of something big. I didn't know HOW big this was going to be. I had no idea. I just knew I needed to be around Pastor Hannah, his anointing, leadership, personality, and character.

I had gotten tired of the van, so I went and bought an Altima. I should have donated the van to the church because I was through paying for it, but I took the van and used it as a down payment on a new car. They had to buy a church van to transport equipment.

I was growing in ministry at that time because I started armor bearing for Pastor Hannah. I was hanging with him a lot, going to hospitals with him and for him. I was going a lot of places for him; police stations on the South Side, and attending different community meetings for him. Places he couldn't go, I went. I needed to be part of something and needed to be involved with him.

One day he had a funeral to do, and he asked me to meet him at the radio station. He wanted me to go with him to the funeral. I caught a bus and met him at the station after he finished the morning show. I rode with him in his car to the funeral.

Pastor Hannah would do different things that would, not surprise me, but confirm that I was right where I needed to be, with him. I would say, yes, I'm with the right person.

We got to the funeral and they didn't have any obituaries. The obituaries were late. He had to do the funeral and the funeral home was ready to start the funeral. The family had to start the funeral without an obituary.

Pastor Hannah found an old obituary in that church and we worked that service from an old obituary of someone else. We went around and found out who was supposed to do what and took the names down. The format for the service came from that old obituary.

He got a pen, standing at the pulpit and said, Brother Cox, you're going to read scripture and you're going to pray, and I'm going to do this part. This was another area where I saw his leadership and saw him take authority. It pulled me in.

When it was time for the eulogy, Pastor Hannah did the eulogy without notes. He had a scripture, he had the little preacher's book, and gave an awesome eulogy with no notes.

We rode to the cemetery for the committal, rode back, and it was just an awesome time.

When we started at the Charles Hayes Center and he was preaching on Sundays, I was there and part of that. I was involved in ministry and always did the after church activities with him too; going to the hospital, praying for people, and house blessings. The more I witnessed his leadership, my respect for him continued to grow.

I was able to practice what I'd learned from him in my full-time job. I began to implement a lot of the qualities that he had because I was speaking and giving presentations. Speaking and empowering people was my job. When I saw him do things, it would empower me.

At the church we had different ministries; the children's ministry, the men's ministry, and the women's ministry. During the holiday season, he would throw a party for each ministry. At that time, it was a small group, so everyone was almost in every ministry. We would go around to visit each ministry party.

That's how the Servants' Christmas party came about. It became one big party.

I used to be Pastor Hannah's armor bearer and it was different because I hadn't been in that atmosphere before. He was mature because he came up in church. He knew a lot already about servitude. When he was coming up in church, I was using dope somewhere.

Pastor Hannah had been the armor bearer for his former pastor, so he knew how to be treated and what the armor bearer was supposed to do. He was teaching me how to serve. He taught me how serve him, and in doing that, I was better able to serve the church. My service started when we picked up that equipment and set up things for worship. That really blessed me to be able to do that for him and for the ministry.

The ministry grew and my sons were acting up. I had to tell Pastor, "I can't go with you like I used to. I have to keep an eye on my boys."

They were getting older and acting up and acting out. I needed to save them.

Pastor Hannah taught me leadership, how to walk in authority and have authority. Even with the challenges I have now, I have nothing but great things to say about how he leads and builds others up to lead. You have to know what areas you need to grow. Some of his sermons seem like they're just for me and others are directed to leadership. The sermons are for everyone, but there are certain sermons that speak directly to me and my situation.

There was a time when I had to pull back from Pastor Hannah. I prayed, God, I want to be there for him. The Lord said, have a heart for him. I wanted to continue to serve as his armor bearer, but I had to take care of my family. God gave me a heart for him.

When new people came to the church, Pastor Hannah would place some of them in positions. There were times when I thought I should have been in that position, but, I wouldn't go anywhere. I decided to stay, and wouldn't let anyone run me away. I had to become okay when he was positioning different people for different reasons and different purposes. The reality was, I was mad, but what these people were being positioned for, I knew nothing about. I had to come to grips with that.

Pastor always says, whatever we need is in the House. God's going to send the people to the House to meet the need. God was doing that, but I was getting mad, wondering why were they getting a position and they just got there, and I'd been there all along?

I had to wrestle with that attitude of being passed over as Pastor Hannah positioned others. They were put in positions to do some things that were not my expertise.

God was sending professionals who were experts in particular areas. They needed to be there and came at the right time. I didn't understand what God was doing at that time.

I had to stay in my position, know MY role, who I was to him and who I was to the church. I eventually learned to accept people, welcome them and appreciate whatever gifts and talents they held.

Some people don't know how to go to the hospital, be with the sick and pray for them and be there with their family, or support someone at a funeral. I used to go to funerals on Pastor's behalf and speak to the family from the pulpit. I was honored to be filling in for the man of God, and I would say just that. I am honored...

I tell the ministers this today. When you go to a family's house or when you go to a funeral, and you're representing New Life Covenant, please use this tag line: It's an honor to stand here on the behalf of Pastor John Hannah, who desired to be here, but was unable to be here. The people welcome us even more when we say that we're standing in for him.

I tell them, when you go to a hospital, to say, "On behalf of Pastor Hannah, Sister Hannah, and the other leaders, I'm here to support the family with prayer and whatever you need."

We're serving God, the church and we're serving him. We want the family to know he sent someone he trusts that will do what he wants done.

I continued to grow and my attitude changed about others coming in getting positions. It didn't bother me anymore. I knew my gifts and talents and was no longer jealous or envious of their talents.

As a leader, and one of the ministers who has been there from the beginning, I began to grow and watch my anointing, what I did and who I was with. I know there's a special kind of love Pastor Hannah has for his members. I don't have to be with him and up under him all the time. He knows that I've been there for a while. I don't expect to be treated differently. I don't try to bogart or thug my way into stuff. Everyone who is new in security, I make sure that they know me. I'll do that.

If a person is around Pastor Hannah enough, they will grow. He speaks to different committees and he speaks to leaders once a month. It's about growth, showing us how to have his heartbeat, knowing how he does things. He's groomed leaders by being around them.

That's the kind of leader Pastor Hannah has been. He doesn't just tell you how to lead; he shows you how to lead, and shows you how to have a heart for people as you lead them. It's been great being under his leadership, to see the excellence, order and the structure he's shown us.

As the church grew, I had to learn to limit the committees and ministries I was on. I had to learn I don't have to be involved in everything.

As a leader, we have to make room for other people to come in and lead. If you still have that same leader in that same position, other people who are ready to serve won't think they have a chance, because somebody is already there. I had to learn to pull back and let other people get involved and try not to be in everything just because I'd been at the church a long time.

When I came to Pastor Hannah, I had about thirteen years of sobriety. I had already worked on a lot of personal healing.

I've been with him over ten years and I'm twenty three years clean. I'm honored to be in the position I'm in now.

It took us awhile to be ordained as ministers, and I understand why. Pastor Hannah was protective of the church and he still is. He said something once, like, "I'm a pastor, but I'm growing. Stay here and let me grow into my pastoral position."

Some people were leaving because they were jealous, envious, thought they should have been put up at certain times, thought that they should have been ordained as ministers, and they left.

Pastor Hannah was growing because he was a young pastor. We were flying the plane as we were building it. I was determined to watch him grow as a pastor and not leave the experience he was getting.

As men, we were growing in some of the same areas together, in the manhood stage and in the marriage stage too. I told myself, you need to stay here and watch how things unfold, stay here without getting into any chaos. I limited my involvement with people (still, to this day) because I didn't want to be involved in any church mess.

When my son died, my wife was out of the church for a while. She just wasn't ready to come back. I continued to come to church without my wife, even after that happened.

I would go to church, get on the altar, pray for my wife, and go home. I would take her out to eat or go to the show. The next week I would ask if she was going to church and she said, no. I would go to church, worship, go home, eat dinner, and take my wife out. This happened for a year or year and a half.

Saturday night I would get her clothes together and ask her if she was going to church. Do you want to wear this? This would look nice on you. She said, no. I said, okay.

I kept praying for her and when she got ready to come back to church, she came back. And the slate was clean. She didn't have to step over any mess when she came back.

Pastor Hannah did a sermon where he had a lot of trash on the stage and there were men dressed in protective suits and helmets with lights.

My wife didn't have to step over any trash to get to me. No one could say, Brother Cox did this, and he did that, while you were gone. There were no scandals, no chaos while she was gone, because I didn't get involved. I do that to this day.

Some people don't want to be involved in all of the duties of ministry. They just wanted to preach. That's why some of them left. They didn't stay to see Pastor Hannah growing as a pastor. He was protective of the church. The church was young, he was young, and he had every right to be protective of the church. I get it. I understand why he didn't let people come in and preach from that pulpit. You can't have everybody on the stage preaching stuff that ain't for the House. I get that.

Pastor Hannah wants to make sure people don't get taken advantage of and that they get the right message that they need to hear.

I had to understand that he was growing and maturing and had to learn how to give up some stuff and not have his hand in everything as a leader because he was overprotective of who should get what. I get it.

It's good. I've gained a lot in ministry and leadership. I've stayed involved and have learned not to take things personal or feel paranoia, thinking he doesn't want me there anymore because other things are taking place.

I named The Temple Project. All the leaders were coming up with names. I said, "Why not just call it, The Temple Project?" A light went off. That's it!

I'm determined to see this Temple built. Pastor asked everyone to pledge. My wife and I paid off our pledge before the time was up.

Pastor wants the people who have been there since the beginning to see this to the end. I've seen people come and go and come back again. I've seen people leave mad, angry and disappointed.

People want to tell Pastor, you should do this, you should do that, trying to present things to him prematurely. Then they get mad when he doesn't okay it. It's not time for him, and it's not time for the House yet.

Before we had the first Bible Study, one Saturday, Pastor Hannah and I did the first outreach for the church. We had some flyers made for the first Thursday night Bible Study. We stood on 39th and Pershing, where the projects were, plugging the first Thursday Bible Study. I'd met him at the condo where he and Anna lived, and before we left, he asked me to pray. I stood at the door praying. It was something like, "God, I pray that if anybody's been looking for him or looking for a church, I pray, in the Name of Jesus, that they will begin to find him and will come..."

I was praying about the church and about people coming to the Bible Study.

We were walking down this block and a lady who knew him from the radio says, "I heard you're starting a church. Where is it going to be?" We gave her the flyer, and after we walked a few more blocks, we went back to his house and ate.

Pastor Hannah said, "Brother Cox, do you see how God answered that prayer?"

Before I met Pastor Hannah, I would pray, but I wasn't looking for the answer or the outcome. He taught me that day, to not only pray without ceasing, but to expect and look for your outcome. I'd never known that.

I've always prayed for my family and for drug addicts and their recovery. "God, I pray for drug addicts, that You get them clean, get them sober, send them to treatment. Thank You every day for my recovery, thank You for my kids, don't let anything happen to my kids." It was a basic prayer. But, when I prayed with him that Saturday morning and we came back, he reminded me that God answered my prayer.

The first Bible Study was overwhelming because we had done outreach in that community and other people Pastor Hannah knew showed up too. A couple hundred people showed up to that first Bible Study. It was awesome. It was awesome!

Pastor Hannah was very instrumental in helping me not only pray for what I want, but to look for and expect the outcome from God.

I learned so much from my pastor and from the church; being a leader of my family, and a leader at work. What I didn't learn from the church, I learned from the 12 Step Program.

LOSING A DREAM

"Sometimes the dream will change unexpectedly. How you cope with the loss will determine if you will dare to dream again."

- HATTIE TREADWELL COX

When my son was killed, that was the first death of our small church in April of 2004. We had just moved to the Charles Hayes Center for Sunday services. We still had Thursday Bible Study at the Blackwell AME church. Pastor Hannah preached my son's funeral.

I literally prophesied my son's death and I didn't know it until Pastor Hannah told me.

Before my son got killed, his older brother and I were with him in the car on a Friday afternoon, about 11:30am or 12:00pm. He'd been out of jail two weeks, but I saw him slipping back. I was taking him to the Secretary of State to get his ID.

I told him, "Son, you just got out of jail. It looks like you're hanging back with that same crowd. Why don't you let me get you in a program, because I don't want you to become a statistic and get killed on the streets. I'm going to cry, I'm going to mourn, but I'm going to have to move on."

He said, "Aww, Dad, it's okay. If it's me, just put me on some Air Force Ones and a jersey and I'll be okay."

(This was the gear at that time, Air Force Ones, jerseys, and blue jean shorts). A silence came over the car.

We arrived to the Secretary of State on North Avenue and Mannheim, and they would not give my son his state ID because he did not have mail with his address on it. We left. That was prophetic to me too. The message I got from that: this was not his home.

Pastor Hannah had an armor bearer named Pastor T. When my son got out of jail, I asked him to come go to church with me. I took him to Pastor Choco's church. They were having church at Clemente High School. I took my son there on a Sunday and they had an altar call. Pastor T. was one of the pastors praying during altar call. When my son went to the altar, Pastor T. prayed for him and led him to the Lord, two weeks before he got killed.

Friday, the lady wouldn't give him an ID because he didn't have a mailing address. The next time I saw him was Monday night, with six bullets in him.

I remember my son on the stone, on the ground, with a sheet over him. During all of that, I stayed sober, still worshiping God, still going to the church, which was still growing. I couldn't get out of my position because I needed the church and the church needed me. I didn't say God needed me. I was there when the church started and they needed me to be a pillar of the church. It was a give and take. I needed to be in a place where I could come to the altar, worship and cry out to the Lord. I had to stay clean and couldn't do any dope. I needed more of God.

It was challenging to work that out and be active in church. I had my moments. It challenged my character and stability, being drug free and not backsliding. My wife stayed out of the church two years after that happened. When she came back, she didn't have to step over any mess that I did while she wasn't there.

After that, I was meeting with Pastor every month, then every three months, and now, it's every six months. It's been good.

A member's son got shot up and was at Cook County Hospital. They called me to go to the hospital and pray for him. I prayed with him and asked God, since my son died, give me this one. Don't take him. I prayed and prayed. He lived. He called and thanked me.

It was a process keeping the family together in the loss of a son. My aunt who raised me had a son who was killed in 1973 or 1975. When my mom died, my aunt raised me. I literally saw my life living out like her life did. I'm her next generation, then my son was killed on the streets of Chicago. She buried most of her siblings. I buried most of my siblings. We were living the same life, trying to keep the family together when tragedy strikes in the home, trying to hold things together and go on without knowing how everyone is doing and feeling.

I wanted to make sure my other sons didn't retaliate. I didn't want them beating up and killing someone else' child because someone killed their brother. They didn't want to hear the God stuff. They were teenagers. My son was 20 when he was killed. That incident almost separated me and my wife. We went through a time. It was challenging as a father to hold things together in the midst of a crisis and trauma. Back to back deaths. My sister died one year, next year, my brother died, the next year, my son got killed. Back to back to back to back. Wow.

Trauma can be the death of a loved one, a child leaving home because they've decided they no longer want to be there anymore, someone getting injured, or the sole provider losing a job when they were paying all of the expenses. This can wipe a family out spiritually, emotionally and financially. I've been there, losing a job because a program folded from lack of funding, still trying to manage a household and look for employment. I had to cut back on unnecessary spending.

When my son was murdered, I let everyone grieve and go through the anger, grief and the acceptance. You have to know how to deal with people when they're grieving. I asked everyone if they were okay. I didn't ask them about therapy, but went and got a therapist for myself because I needed to be strong for them. I probably should have suggested counseling for them too.

It's important to know what your outlet is. Is it writing? Is it running? Is it dancing? At that time, I didn't know what I needed. I needed to talk to a psychiatrist. They gave me medication and it didn't work, so I didn't take it. Individual weekly counseling worked for me, not medication. I had the individual counseling once a week, a support group, friends, and a men's group. We met weekly, ate, and talked about our issues. That's what I needed in that season of my life.

Know what you need for the season you are in. That's important, whether it's a financial situation or health, or losing someone or losing a job. It was a challenge that the oldest kids were doing what they wanted to do and the youngest kids were following them. We had to let them know they couldn't keep doing what they were doing because the others were doing it too. I couldn't lose control of the house, so they had to be checked. A couple of times they had to leave. They were not going run the house and damage everyone else. When I'm damaged, I have to make sure I'm not causing damage somewhere else because I'm not getting my needs met.

Make sure you take care of yourself so you can be ready for the challenges ahead. Then see what others need to get through the crisis. Make sure they know you value their feelings.

TURNING 50

In January 2013, I experienced anxiety because I was turning 50 in October of that year. I would wake up in a sweat. My mother, father, two brothers and sister never made it to 50. In August, God reminded me that I was already in my 50th year. I was waiting on October to hit 50. I threw a party but should have let someone else handle it. I invited 150 people, but only 50 showed up. I still broke ground on new territory. Nobody else in my family had been able to throw a 50th birthday party.

I woke up many nights, afraid to go to sleep, scared I might not wake up.

It was a big fear that I was living each day. I was not looking at the victory and should have been thanking God and blessing Him to let me see 50, but I was too overwhelmed about what was going to happen, instead of seeing that God used me to set a new path in my blood line.

Turning 50 was really hard for me. I remember when I turned 49. In February, I met with Pastor Hannah and I told him how I was feeling. Instead of him being sad with me, he said "Well, throw yourself a party!" He said, "Celebrate." So, I started planning a 50th birthday party in February for October. I started saving, putting money away, trying to make it happen.

The week before that, Pastor Hannah was preaching about the prodigal son's oldest brother. You can have your own party. You're waiting for the father to throw a party, but you can have your own party. I'm like, wow! My family never did it, so I did it. I started preparing to do it, but I tried to do it on my own instead of hiring someone to organize the whole thing.

I was selective of the people I invited and I should have just opened it up. I didn't get the outcome that I expected, and I spent a nice piece of money on it. I had a hall and a live band and wanted people to enjoy themselves. Those who showed up, showed up. The most important message was that I broke a pattern. I made it to 50, I saved the money and threw a party.

I haven't seen anyone in my family model what I'm trying to do. It's a blessing to see what God has done for me and what He's doing in my life.

That's what turning 50 was for me. It was really challenging and it was hard for me to walk in the victory because there was a fear of walking in victory.

In a couple of months, I'll be 51, so God has really been doing some great things in my life. I'm accepting and owning up to where I am. I'm grateful. I have to keep remembering that He's been blessing me.

I experienced mid-life crisis moments; the anxiety of dying, wondering if I was going to reach 50. God has blessed me beyond 51. He's left me here to be a blessing to others. You have a purpose too. Find out what that is, and walk in it.

PERSONAL INTEGRITY

"Standing tall and proud won't matter in the results. Standing firm guarantees your growth."

- Gregory Cox

People should see your integrity in every setting so that you will make an impact wherever you go. You can't behave one way over here and be seen out of character somewhere else. It's important to remain consistent.

When people respect your integrity, they welcome your participation in various personal and professional groups. I like to get to programs and luncheons early to see how the keynote speaker addresses their audience, and to learn how the event has been organized.

You've heard the saying, it's not how you start, but how you finish. I'm just trying to finish well.

I check out the agenda before putting in my two cents. I've worked for a lot of social service agencies. Their vision and mission may be different, but the bottom line, they're trying to have the same results, to better individuals, families and communities.

CURRENT SITUATION, THEN AND NOW

> "Who needs Happily Ever After, when sharing my success with others feels good right now?"
>
> - Hattie Treadwell Cox

I'm doing things and meeting people I never thought I would meet. I have been in positions that I didn't feel I deserved, and didn't know how to walk in it. I was seeing people and going places I never thought I'd go. I was doing better than I expected, trying to fit in positions, even though low self esteem was saying I wasn't supposed to be there because this had never happened to anyone in my family or to anyone close to me.

I had feelings of incompetency, like I didn't know what I was doing. I was speaking in front of people with big degrees, doctors, police officers, firemen, and professionals. I didn't have a degree and felt like I wasn't qualified to tell them anything.

My pastor always says some of us have jobs we're not qualified for. I'm getting to a place I never thought I would see and am in positions that I never thought would be mine.

When I got off dope in 1991, I just wanted to get off dope and didn't have in my mind I would be speaking to anybody about staying clean or about getting their kids back. I didn't see any of that. I just wanted to stop using dope, stop the pain from withdrawing, and I wanted my boys back.

My current situation has me in a position where I'm able to empower and educate professionals and birth parents. The current situation is good. When you're doing what you're supposed to do, it feels good to be in this position. It feels great.

It's good that people know you and speak to you, and you don't have a clue who they are. I know people in church, in social service and the 12 Step community. It's good I can meet people and my integrity is still intact. I'm not doing one thing in one place and doing something else in another place.

CLICKING THE LINKS

Have you ever opened up an email, and it gave you a website? You went to that website, and inside that page there's another website to another page, and then another in that, and you keep clicking and clicking, on and on? Before you know it, you've gone so far from the first website where you started and probably didn't get a chance to finish the first article, because something encouraged you to go to another website to find out more. What good is that? In doing research, that's good, but sometimes you shouldn't wander off before it's time. You shouldn't do other things before you complete what you started, what's in front of you.

My mind can wander off thinking about other things and I have to come back to my current situation because I will worry myself about things and it will get me away from my current, where I am filled with gratitude. I've been delivered 23 years, been married 20 years, raised over 10 kids, have grandkids and I'm working. My current situation is good. I shouldn't be wandering off, worrying, murmuring and complaining about other stuff. I have to come back. It's like trying to start two or three businesses and the first one is not doing well. Don't wander off your current situation.

__Life can hit you pretty hard. Learn from it, stay focused, don't wander off, and you'll find the end of the road.__

ADVOCATING FOR OTHERS

"Empowering others begins with
self-advocacy."

- Hattie Treadwell Cox

An advocate is one who supports another or a cause. I'm committed to advocating for birth parents involved with the child welfare system who are trying to reunite with their family. It's important to strengthen yourself before you're able to advocate for others.

Birth parent is a term used by DCFS (Department Of Children And Family Services) to describe parents who are involved in child welfare. I get calls from birth parents who are just getting started in the journey that I completed. They're frustrated, angry, disappointed, baffled and confused. These are just some of the emotions. Birth parents are being referred to me by caseworkers because I've already experienced the process. I'm honored to receive calls from birth parents. The first thing I tell them is that I'm not a lawyer. They want me to sort out some of the confusion and contradictions, when they don't understand what is happening in the system. I'm honored to be in this position of being an advocate. How did I get here?

When I started this journey I just wanted to make a life change, get my kids back and be the best father I could be. I didn't set out to be an advocate or ever think of being an advocate for anyone or anything.

When I got my life together, I was able to work with birth parents who were trying to reunite with their family and stay sober. This included working with parents who were trying to regain custody while they struggled with multiple issues. I shared with them what worked for me, and hoped they would use the information if they needed it. I suggested they address the problems and issues that brought the case into the system. For those who experienced addictions, they would have to remain sober and drug free.

I've had the opportunity to meet professionals in this field who admired me and the courage God gives me to pour out and do what I'm doing.

I'm honored to still be here. I've known parents who have gotten clean and sober, relapsed, and given up on the process of fighting to get their children back. Then their kids went back into the system from them relapsing, which resulted in a new child welfare case from neglect or abuse. Early on, I didn't see what I was doing as great, but now, I see the importance of helping other birth parents reunite with their children.

I'm glad to be able to fight for a cause that's important. There are so many African-American kids in the system. They need the support, so I want to continue the work that I'm doing in being an advocate. I have to stay educated on the current data, language and the temperature of the child welfare system.

Concerning the budget, I need to know if they're cutting services for birth parents. If so, that's not good. If you're cutting their services, then they're not trying to help the children be returned home. You're moving more toward adoption than reunification.

There's a thin line between entitlement, what you think you should have or what you're supposed to have. I tell birth parents to advocate and stand up for themselves in the midst of whoever is around them. They have to get their needs met sometimes.

I'm not a confrontational person, not in terms of physical fighting, but being able to have a healthy debate is okay. I've been passive, humble and let things go, but, I'm starting to speak up more now. These are speaking points I share with birth parents.

Some birth parents don't know how to ask for what they need. I tell them to make a list of what they need. There's a spirit of inferiority that happens with some birth parents around people with authority, because they sense a spirit of superiority and they're shut down. So they walk away without having a clear understanding of the family court system and the process. If they address their needs instead of sweeping it under the rug, they will get what they want.

Unfortunately, I'm unable to be with birth parents at every stage. When they come in, they're at an angry stage and I haven't been able to peel off the layers so that they are able to receive, so I can deposit into them. They're fragile, vulnerable, weak, they don't know or understand, so I have to take my time with them to get them to a place of acceptance, whether it was their fault or not.

Sometimes it's not their fault. Parents may have left their children with a family member, and the family member left the children home alone, and DCFS came and took the kids. The parent may have gone to a job interview and not understand why the kids were removed by DCFS. The decision made to leave them with family was okay but it was damaging that the family member left them home alone. The parent is saying it's not their fault; the family member did it. But DCFS will say, you left the children with them. They feel they're not bad parents because they did not leave the children alone. But because the family member did it, the parents have to participate in services and complete a service plan to reunite with their family.

ADVOCATING WITH THE RIGHT INFORMATION

You have to know the purpose of the advocacy. I tell them I can only assist them with information to help them understand their rights as a birth parent. If their rights aren't being met, they need someone to speak up for them. They're vulnerable and trust has to be built. They have to trust me and know that I'm not part of the system. In their eyesight, everyone who looks professional is against them. To lighten the load, I introduce myself as a birth parent, telling them my story, and that helps bring their guard down. When their guards are brought down, I've penetrated a wall, and the trust comes. I tell them things that I know they don't know about their case, such as the purpose of a court hearing. This is some of what I do in advocating for others and teaching them to advocate for themselves.

Being an advocate is closer to me and more important than ever. I wasn't raised with it. My father advocated for dope just like I did. My parents came up in the 50s and 60s and I didn't see my parents fighting for rights. I only saw it on TV.

Advocating is bigger than ever. My concern for the families and children is growing.

My heart is heavy, advocating for people, not just parents, but for those in the church. Praying for other people. My heart is heavy. God is strengthening my compassion, my love and my heart for doing for others. I'm being asked to intercede for others spiritually and professionally.

Being an advocate for someone else is not always easy. I have to get information to the birth parents so they will understand it. If you're trying to communicate with someone, and they didn't get it, you didn't communicate it. It could be tone or delivery. Standing in the gap for others has humbled me. God chose me to be able to do this. It's a load, though. It's not going to let up either. It's got me seeking the strength to continue to do what I'm doing. It's okay. I'm advocating in areas where I've overcome and knowing the purpose of my advocacy.

Like Moses wandering in the wilderness 40 years, I don't want to make a crazy decision in the 39th year that will impact all the people I've been advocating for. I'm careful of how I conduct myself around professionals. I advise birth parents about their appearance, and having a healthy attitude when they go to court. When I see them do that, it's gratifying because it lets me know I'm on the right track. Use what you have to give it to others and help them grow so that they will be able to tell their story.

One of the main reasons why I do what I do is because I've been able to sustain from alcohol and drugs with a support system that's still effective to this day. Take advantage of the resources available to you.

QUITTING IS NOT AN OPTION

"At some point, it's not about finishing up with the team. It's about completing the race for your own self-esteem and self-worth."

- Gregory Cox

I've been asked many times: Why didn't I quit, give in or give up with some of my challenges? One of the things I would say is, quitting is not an option. I would rather keep going, and be successful at being a great father, being a good employee or being a good husband. I would rather keep trying to be the best, and keep moving, rather than never know how far I could have gone.

That's the concern of mine when it comes down to quitting altogether. I don't want to get to Heaven and Jesus tell me, you were almost there and you quit.

There were moments when I questioned, what am I doing and why? Is this book going to be impactful? Are people going to read it? Will it be worth reading? Will I see a return on my investment? These are some of the questions.

I need to keep reinventing myself by launching into different types of projects to stay motivated and encouraged. I have to monitor my commitments. Sometimes you have to overproduce in order to get what you want.

I want to get to the finish line. I've seen video clips of races where runners have injured themselves, but they kept running.

I'm trying to meet my goal. I'm trying to be the best me I can be, the best Greg I can be. I'm not trying to be anyone else. I have to keep finding out what I need to motivate me for the next level, next phase, and next success.

I need new challenges because I need new successes. I can't keep riding on old successes even though some of them have motivated me. I have to keep reinventing myself and keep moving forward. This project has helped me do just that.

This book is about creating a new trend for my family, a new road for them to travel. Quitting is not an option. Let's fight to break old patterns to tread on new ground. Let's find new ways to stay focused to get to the finish line.

COURAGE TO SEEK HELP

"Be encouraged as you look for help. Help is looking for you too."

- Gregory Cox

I knew I had a problem after my kids were removed from my home as a result of my drug addiction. Where did I find the courage to seek help? When did I know it was time to seek help?

It was a time of fear. I was terrified that the guy next door was going to do something to me because I owed him money for drugs. Fear of getting hurt helped me make the decision to go get help. The courage came from wanting a better life. I made the call and they told me to come in.

Back in 1991, a bottle of wine was $1.10 and bus fare was $1.10 with a transfer. A transfer lasted a long time back then, three or four rides. I was on the corner asking for some change, and got enough bus fare to go to treatment. It took courage to make a healthy and a wise decision to go to treatment instead of buying a pint of wine. I went to treatment and haven't looked back since then.

I went to treatment for my kids. They were always asking me when they would be able to move back with me, wondering why they had to stay at their grandmama's house.

I told them I was going to get an apartment one day, promising them the moon and couldn't deliver a star. I remembering the looks on their faces. I don't have to put a label on things; I just went to treatment. Someone else labeled it. Today, being spiritual, I can say God ordained me to go to treatment. The courage came from staying in the program, not leaving and walking away, to get the help I needed.

There are areas in my life where I need the courage to ask for help in doing something or completing something. Once, I was working for an agency and it was time for monthly reports and I was behind in getting the last reports done. I asked a coworker to help me. They invited me to their home to help me. I was so worried about what someone would say about me asking for help instead of being humble and knowing my limitations.

I have to know what I can and can't do, admit my limitations and not be led by ego into doing something I know I can't handle. It's important to know your limitations and have the courage to ask for help.

Leadership is about helping others get into the right position to help others for a bigger cause. If you can't do it, find out who can. The Serenity Prayer talks about courage and wisdom. I have to have the wisdom to know what I can't do, and have the courage to ask for help. I have to know my limitations at the job, in a friendship, and a marriage.

I need to know where the ball stops, so I won't dig myself into a hole I can't get out of, trying to appear to be something that I'm not. You must have the courage to acknowledge you need help, receive a referral, and follow up on the referral.

When my wife and I realized we needed to file bankruptcy, we were given a recommendation. We followed up to get help. It took courage and a willingness to follow through. Effective counselors will refer you to someone else if they don't have the answers.

SLIPS AND SETBACKS

> "Avoid the slippery things of life that slide
> you back to the starting gate."
>
> - Hattie Treadwell Cox

Folks get clean for awhile and may have slips and setbacks. The program calls it a relapse. The church calls it backslide. There is a different term depending on the setting you're in. In the recovery community it's called a relapse or a slip.

People ask me why I haven't had a relapse with drinking or drugs. Attending 12 Step meetings and groups was the support that worked for me. I did what I was supposed to do and recognized when I needed additional support. I added to my recovery process by listening to a lot of Christian preachers and reading their books. There were different seasons that strengthened my recovery and sobriety.

I want people who read this book to see that I didn't resist when it was time to mature. Twenty three years later, I have not had a slip or a setback. I attended a monthly men's group. We talked about family, jobs, and career. That men's group is still going on, twenty years later.

Slips and setbacks do happen. You have to ask yourself, what did I stop doing and what more could I have done? You can't be rebellious and say you don't need that, because it could be exactly what you need. It has a lot to do with maturity. When I started using, it was me, me, me, mine, mine, mine. There were always excuses not to buy stuff so I could use more drugs and alcohol. It was all about me.

Are you ready to mature in your deliverance? God will deliver you, but you must mature. Jesus said, go and sin no more. Go and do something different than what you've been doing. (John 8:11c)

I met with a guy who wanted to have his cake and eat it too. He was not willing to sacrifice some of what he wanted to meet the need for someone else, namely, his children. He was gambling compulsively and obsessively and it was at its peak. He was only thinking of himself. I can identify with it because I wanted what I wanted, and had to learn it wasn't about me, but about those kids. When you can admit what's going on, that's a sign of growth.

When I was in the program, some of the guys relapsed and started using drugs again. It scared me. I increased everything I was doing and brought it up a notch.

Now, if I have a lot on my plate and I'm stretched, I start minimizing to avoid burnout. For example, if I have several projects with deadlines, I will prepare one at a time instead of trying to focus on all of them at the same time.

If someone has had a relapse, or fear of relapse, they're falling back into old ways of thinking and behavior. There are people who are clean from drugs, but they're going to the gambling boat, still practicing that compulsive and obsessive behavior. There's a spirit of greed in that and adolescent rebellion. Adolescents want to have their own way, they don't want to clean up; they're obsessed with themselves, what they want, when they want it and how they want it. It's all about me. I've seen this in adults. That's why I haven't had any setbacks.

INSIDE LONG-TERM RECOVERY

"There's no map on how to get there, just tools to make your trip more manageable."

- Hattie Treadwell Cox

I've been sober and clean longer than I used drugs. I used ten or fifteen years but have been clean twenty plus years. You have to address your life issues, loss of loved ones, loss of a job, kids acting up, and conflict in marriage. I started using drugs when I was younger, when things were chaotic in the home. My mother was sick, my older brothers and sisters were acting out, and my father was physically, verbally and spiritually abusive to us.

Inside long term recovery I had to deal with the crises of life and not use drugs. I had to keep going and take care of myself in the midst of whatever was going on. I went to meetings and talked to friends. The tools and strategies I learned from my drug treatment got me where I am today.

What does a person need to recover? First, identify why you use drugs and alcohol. You have to address issues, the crises and not crawl into a corner, saying, forget it, I'm going to get high. That's adolescent behavior.

In long term recovery, be able to identify what you need, when you need it, as long as it improves your personal growth and commitment.

It's important to know what you need and do it for yourself and not have to count on others to do it for you, whether it's going to a movie, a restaurant or a walking around to the store to buy socks or T-Shirts. I had to take care of me.

If I feel like treating someone, I can call a couple of the guys and say let's go out, it's on me. I'm not doing it for them; I'm doing it for me. I just need to be around them and just be Greg. I don't need to be Minister Cox, or Hattie's husband, or Jermaine's father. I need to sit down and be Greg. When I have those Greg moments, I can be me. I can address what's going on with me, what I'm doing, what I wish I hadn't done. I'm able get it all out and address my crises, challenges, goals, dreams, drives, wishes, ambitions, faults, and disappointments. I need to be in a safe place to get that out. After that, I'm good because I've gotten some feedback and I realize it wasn't as bad as I thought it was. That's the growth of long term recovery and being able to address the challenges of life and not revert back into the adolescent behavior.

That's important in leadership too. Can you lead and still be able to address a lot of issues?

Talk about what's going on. Have the courage to address your stuff. Identify and admit where you are, even if it's defeat. Be vulnerable and open yourself up. There's a leadership quality in that. It's not saying, I'm weak, but I'm confident enough to keep moving forward. I'm not going to quit, give up or stop.

That's where I am with the growth of our church. There were times when I wanted to leave, and wondered was it time for me to go, and then I said, I wasn't going anywhere. In staying, I became one of the elders of the church and highly respected. That's good and lets me know I made a healthy decision not to leave, but to stay and see the growth of the church and be the leader that God called me to be.

What you need to recover is a healthy surrounding. You need people around you who are also getting healthy, who want to grow and are not stagnant and stuck in immature behavior.

You need people around you who are at a higher level so you will have something to reach. That's important, to reach for something higher.

I'm amazed at what God is doing in this growth process and my deliverance. He's sending people to me to help them work through some things.

I'm too old to use dope. I can't see me standing in line asking for change, saying I'm short, can I get it on credit and pay you back tomorrow? Do people still do that?

Talking about your issues is healthy because they will no longer have a hold on you. Not sharing or telling anyone about them, causes them to grow. If it's a desire, a craving or an urge, you need to be able to share that.

If it's a man who's thinking of cheating on his wife or a wife who's thinking of cheating on her husband, if it's not shared with anyone, it grows. When it's exposed to light, it can be worked on because it's no longer a hidden secret. That's helpful in recovery, to put it out there and talk about it. In talking about it, God has a way of giving you the answer.

I remember when I got drunk for the first time. I was living in the projects. There were thirteen floors in the projects. I stayed on the second floor and a friend of mine stayed on the first floor. My mother was alive then. I was thirteen and got drunk at his house. Some parents are the type who would say, I'd rather for you to do it here, than out there. My mother was just the opposite, saying, you're not getting high or drinking nothing up in here. So, his house was the place to be. I was so drunk I couldn't even make it upstairs, from the first floor to the second floor.

There was a liquor store on Madison and Oakley. When I was thirteen I was able to pass for seventeen or eighteen. If we weren't able to buy drinks, we could stand on the corner and get someone older to buy it for us.

Me and a friend of mine were the ones sent to get drinks. We all put money up for drinks and we had change left over, so we got a pint of wine to drink on the way back. We figured we could do that since we were the runners. We drank the wine and everything else they had, and got drunk, tore up, and I couldn't make it upstairs. To this day, I don't know how I made it upstairs. I was supposed to tell my mother I was spending the night or ask could I spend the night. I don't remember what happened. That was the beginning of alcoholism for me.

Some situations I willingly got myself into, and some situations I allowed people to pull me into their mess, because I was naïve or people pleasing. It's up to you to participate, or pull back and say, "No, that's it for me. I'm done!"

Resources/Websites

Narcotic Anonymous http://www.na.org/

Alcoholic Anonymous http:// www.aa.org

Cocaine Anonymous http:// www.ca.org

www.bestrongfamilies.net

www.pride-institute.com

www.alcoholanddrugsrehab.com

Domestic Violence www.thehotline.org

Fathers Program www.fatherhood.org

Child Abuse hotline 1-800 25-abuse (22873)

Shelter for the homeless www.pgm.org

ABOUT THE AUTHOR

Gregory Cox has over ten years of professional managerial experience. He is a certified parent instructor and a seasoned public speaker who promotes positive behavior. He has co-authored two books, "The Parents' Get Real Guide to Getting Your Kids Back," and "The Parents' Get Real Guide to Keeping Your Kids at Home." In addition, Gregory has published several articles regarding fathers' rights and responsibilities. He previously served as chairman of the Cook County Birth Parent Council (BPC).

In the spirit of teamwork, he joined other BPC members to present birth parent issues to approximately 150 juvenile court personnel, including state attorneys, bar attorneys, public defenders, and child defense attorneys.

Currently, Gregory Cox is the program coordinator for services involving family and children with a focus on birth parents. He attends DCFS focus groups with DCFS staff and juvenile court officials, and has provided presentations at DCFS Foundations Trainings for newly hired child welfare workers. He is also responsible for developing the concept of an Annual Institute Day. This empowers birth parents with information on navigating the child welfare system. This event has been instituted into the activities of DCFS's Partnering with Parents Initiative.

Gregory Cox is a loving and devoted husband, father, and a faithful servant at one of the largest non-denominational churches in Chicago.

www.ingramcontent.com/pod-product-compliance
Lightning Source LLC
Chambersburg PA
CBHW071459160426
43195CB00013B/2156